Hegemonick

Also by Andrew Jordan:

St Catherine's Buried Chapel (Taxus, 1987)
The Mute Bride (Stride, 1998)
Ha Ha (Shearsman, 2007)
Josian in Ermonie (bending oeuvre, 2009)
Bonehead's Utopia (Smokestack, 2011)

Andrew Jordan

Hegemonick

Shearsman Books

First published in the United Kingdom in 2012 by
Shearsman Books Ltd
50 Westons Hill Drive
Emersons Green
Bristol
BS16 7DF

Shearsman Books Ltd Registered Office
30–31 St. James Place, Mangotsfield, Bristol BS16 9JB
(this address not for correspondence)

www.shearsman.com

ISBN 978-1-84861-220-4

Some parts of this book have previously appeared, or will appear, in
Blart, Great Works, the text

Cover Photograph: 'Hark, Hark, the Lark at Heaven's Gate Sings'
by Ida A. Battye (from *The English Landscape in Picture, Prose
and Poetry*, Ed. Kathleen Conyngham Greene, published by Ivor
Nicholson & Watson Ltd, London 1932).

Designed by Andrew Jordan.

Contents

Part One: The Sonnet Past

The Bull Artefact

[*artefact inscription*]
A worm of many features
A colossus of tiny worms
[All eyes and mouths]
Collision of myth and genetic
marvels • Beast of many heads
Colossal thighs • Huge buttocks
This invisible majesty
she sings sweetly • this head
that emerges from a hole
in the ground • it sings
Hands everywhere • Nightie
pulled up • Heraldic autopsy
Surgical exhibition • I saw
the calm exterior • Tradition
Fields • Trees • A path where
the worm wriggled back into
her mouth • Eyes of forearm
Eyes of the palm • The closed eye
of the nipple she reveals • Eye
of tongue • Inside the beast
"all gothed up" • a host synapse

Cortex technicality • Neural
networks • ions • In the mirror
there are scales—tiny wings
and [all over her body] these
blank despairing eyes.

The Paulsgrove Experiment

A mast or tower inside an enclosure.
This is what it was like then, I said
"It looks like an idol, the head of a bull."
A test rig, canvas draped on scaffolding,
about it many obsolete fortifications,
buttress and bastion, a bulwark built for the
defence of the past. I had it in my mind
to walk up to the tower, to look down
into the gardens, to see the houses below,
the shops and flats a colossus bends to inspect.
Paedophile thoughts were beamed into the estate.
Relax she said your limbs relax and breathe.
Allurements, coercive rewards, false claims;
of course some fell for it. I had a strong desire
to confess, to clear myself from all my harms.
And then it went and identified clusters and
who was in them; from ordinary homes
it told me they monitored nodes in the network.
It wasn't just us spreading rumours. It said
to me by means of mathematical modelling
where new labyrinths were formed they saw it
and where old tunnels opened up they knew.
From up there they looked down on us
and we enacted it. *Echolalia.* I had this thing
about an ancient moon goddess for days,
she called my name, said *let your mind
roam free.* Go through the science to the bull in
the maze, *Qinetiq.* Remember how, in the past,
we had furtive or private lives, the things
we cared about and then lost hold of.

Obsolete fortifications. Their ramparts embody the way
collective or national power has become a re-enactment
of itself within an illusion called 'transparency'. Powers
dispersed through sentiments, our sense of the past. Pain and
remission from pain underpins our interest in heritage.

MOD PROPERTY - PHOTOGRAPHS PROHIBITED

This where there is nothing to see. The turf is eerily smooth—
or in the distance rucked and bumped
where the remains of structures poke through.

Pasture of muniments. It monitors their phones.

The private person is compared with the personas

they present, their observable behaviour. Strident

or furtive, they are known. Outer compliance and

inner withholding of compliance: this is the fracture

the State must fill, into which it already extends.

Qinetiq and Dstl (Defence Science and Technology Laboratory) were created in
2001 when the government divided the original cult into two colleges. Dstl is the
publicly owned research organisation. Qinetiq is the privatised 'shop window'.

Qinetiq works to a "global customer base" and offers "technology rich services and
solutions". Enclosures used by the cult are mostly not marked on Ordnance Survey
maps. The most famous centre of cult operations is Porton Down in Wiltshire.

There is a long history of weapons research on Portsdown Hill. It is a tradition
continued to this day in compounds first enclosed during the Neolithic period.
Many new or experimental weapons are based on prehistoric originals unearthed,
it is said, from the very barrows upon which today's research facilities are located.
What was once considered 'magical' is now merely 'state of the art'.

The prototype 'Bull Artefact' was raised from just such a site.

Hypnophrenia

A poem was transmitted into my head
or my poem was broadcast over the landscape. †

I walked into The Churchillian
and everyone stopped talking
and the girl behind the bar said, "Oh you're here—
we've been expecting you . . ."

The whole place was lit up
by light off the sea, the horizon was
silvered. I sat by a window
and endured the glare. I felt like a component
on a circuit board, a transistor.

As directed, I took out my notebook
and began to write—I channelled
involuntary imagery, invasive thoughts
called 'inspirations'.

She interrupted me: ". . . of course
you should be pleased," she said,
"you have broken through a block
and these affects are natural, a part
of the healing process. That's why you came."

I was crawling along a tunnel that linked one complex
of fears to another deep in my neurosis. I did not know
this part of my body—this tunnel that will go on forever
with no opening out into the chamber . . .

---

† The poem referred to is The Sonnet Past.

"You see," she said, "how you are exploring
neural pathways, precious veins, energy lines . . ."

She said we must LIBERATE THE SACRED GROVE
to cure the phobias I had known
as a part of my self since I had lived
on Portsdown Hill, over an emptiness—
the chambers of the heart, the miles of tunnels
that make up the body— where
I had walked too close to the fences at night,
becoming drawn by shooting stars and strange
pulses of light over the research establishments.

Helicopter movements, there were objects
in the night sky to ensure a new dawn.

My hypnotherapist was Dstl trained.
I think she told me this and then told me to forget.
She set the conditions
under which I recollect her, or parts of her.

She had worked for them. Through a process of healing
she concealed her own thoughts inside my body,
left me to wander through her neuroses in my dreams,
feel how they connected to mine, forming centres
of consciousness deep below the hill that I must find.

She tuned me to the frequencies, placed codes
of her own within my flesh, made the muniments
work differently, as if they were a part of me—
she used my numb dissociation to embody
experimental technologies, pleasures
and rewards and meanings to strengthen me . . .

And when I realised and tried to contact her
she didn't answer her phone
and her listing had vanished
from the Hypnotherapy UK web site.
They said they'd never heard of her.

She made my being subsidiary to hers—she became
my meaning—stored her self in my own for safe keeping;
she left the map inside my body, so that I know my heart
is a location inside Portsdown Hill;
she betrayed her employers, used me as her mule,
and then she disappeared. Recalled to head office,
she is filed in deep calcareous fissures. *She is gone.*

There were suggestions.

A sound like shouting through the wall.

I could not sleep.

The lines I followed led me to Portsdown Hill,
past the house where I had lived as a teenager,
the location of despair, and up into the dazzling light,
that extraordinary view, where the insights began.

The Sonnet Past

There was a raised causeway: *an atmosphere, a depth.* [1]
This might have been a Roman road. Present time
came through the outer world of antiquity, *a steep hill angled
on a coomb* an unavoidable utopia.

    Our point of view
    is manufactured in
    the odd perspective
    of these days. [2]

In the distance the city dump beside the motorway
where the past is contained in a crucible of earth.
Unclean narrative. We watch from timelessness,
preservation, stillness. We can see Public Art—
those ludicrous sails between the carriageway and dump,
which might have been placed to entrap the energy
spill of cars, their endless murmuring. [3]
Heritage is a form of amnesia. [4] After the Reformation
there's nothing to remember. With heritage, objects
do it for you, the past is just the bit you consume.

    There was a storm
    of Time in the night.
    A vast black spiral
    lifted rooves, erasing

    things, it uprooted
    trees in the park.
    Decades tore through
    the woods, nulled futures

from the otherworld,
or its absence,
removing whole tracts
of memory, leaving

blank views through
the new cognition
(evoke   )
and Psyche Woods

---

[1] Cancer of power—the line of tension
a swelling in the earth; tubercle, embossment,
a stud platform from under which to measure
and survey the machine called Time
they had discovered and explored. A cameo
on the printed page, a clock made of money.

[2] This prominence to show the ages of man
and woman as a flatness—horizontal planes
of non-history under the Romance—stunning
finds of giant bones beneath them, the
lizard spread—like a drawing on the chalk—

[3] once worshipped; a tableaux of beasts
and this her teat *Apollyon* over
a pattern of ribs. Simultaneity & the vortex. Titania
leading an incubus into the distance—a blur
or dazzle into which you cannot see.

[4] (*Ex patria, ex sonnet*; Portsea Island was always a world apart.
An ancient funerary grove, the place of British Pyramids
and life everlasting (see *Tricorn, Hilsea Triangle*, etc.). Here the
princes were raised to have no sense of direction. They sailed
to all points at once. From this absence of perspective
the mainland is the otherworld or the Land of the Dead
and so it remains—Cosham is the portal and you go up hill
into her body via Purbrook, there are buses or you can walk.)

Part Two: A Paulsgrove Bestiary

Equus

We missed our stop at Portchester. Absorbed
in the map—an alignment pointed out
between St Mary's church, the Norman keep
and the entrance to the tunnel in the hill. †
Fort Nelson. An impression of gloom above
exposed gardens—the lines of sodden washing—
and fields of Wimpey homes. Suffocation.
A bleak acreage that lost itself in fog.
The cloud is low today. We pass
Wymering church, an outpost amongst pagans.
Their mysterious loss of being—still
rectified in this squat aspect of faith,
like a hard truth to learn—luminous
at the centre of the thicket. Innocence
cowering amongst the scabby thorns
where once even the incumbent
was a paedophile. Paulsgrove, a vast,
betrayed estate—like an otherworld—
surrounding it. We got off at Cosham.
Our rendezvous, the White Hart at Portchester,
already lost. The key to the riddle
in which 'how you feel in your body'
is the map that shows you the way out.

---

† Portsdown Hill, an east/west oriented escarpment north of
Portsmouth. The St Mary's referred to is in Fratton Road, Portsmouth.
The alignment extends across Portsmouth Harbour, passing through
St Mary's, Portchester, the keep of Portchester Castle and then up to
the gate of Fort Nelson, our intended destination.

The line continues on to St Nicholas church, Wickham. Of Wickham,
the *New Hampshire Village Book* (Hampshire Federation of Women's
Institutes, 1990) states, "Wickham was the birthplace of William of
Wykeham, Bishop of Winchester and founder of Winchester College,
in the 14th century. The mound on which the church is built was used
by Celts and Saxons for burial or religious rites. St Nicholas was built
by the Normans in the 12th century . . ."

She was pure in hers. Now, mutilated,
his white mare bleeds iron oxide on the hill—
and his gentle sacrifice must be made—
a spiritual urge *domesticated*
and under the knife. † A form of planning
with an outcome. *Chakra.* A burst bin at Cosham.
My lifeline leading me astray
along Portsdown Hill, into Paulsgrove
where they burn witches and some still light
the wicker man upon the green
which is at the heart of the design
of this 'garden city' environment,
this experiment in prefabricated culture.
The beast in us penned in—fingering
the lock—gone tribal. PFC. *Pompey,
in heaven's light.* The moon and sun.
It is written on the massive
concrete abutment beneath the motorway.
Alembic of good fortune, crucible of the soul;
the *working class*, unhitched from a reality
not really made by them, nor owned,
but an ideal that served to fill the gaps
left in identity. We walked through the ideal,
from Self Help into Loathing, where
disgust is palpable. Each public space—
an anxiety. Hatred as *the* utility that links
unredeemed social housing—the human trash—

---

† A reference to the Hampshire Horse Ripper, who may live in the Paulsgrove area.
Conventionally assumed to be a lone male, he attacked horses throughout
Hampshire over many years—genitally mutilating them—possibly for ritual
purposes. Despite a lengthy police operation and fearful vigilance from horse
owners no-one was ever charged with these offences. In recent years, as far as
I know, there have been no reported attacks.

to those who benefit and own.
Paedophile, they cannot spell it but they know
it's wrong. A last ditch to defend against
the beast that lurks behind the eyes
that look at little girls and boys.
The self in the mirror. Witch. *Seducer.*
Seeing my own destructive potential
in a grain of sand—the beast
in what blocks me. *Righteous boy.*
Sullen glare. Walk past the shop, a mass
of graffiti spelling death to outsiders.
Don't look back. Once more, to discourse
on the council estate as an image
of Eden. Drunken teenager, belching,
and his girlfriend's exposed midriff—
her thong pulled up so high
above the waistband of her jeans
that you can see what you must not look at.
Greenfields Meats. The Co-op. Outside,
a boy still young enough to play
on the floor to look up ladies skirts.
A late beehive bobbing by. The last Ted
in these parts lived here. *Pause.*
The bank of the motorway, located
to provide atmosphere—a kind of fosse—
an ancient affect which might unite
the tribe around children—their innocence
plastered over the slope as *fool's parsley,*
toadflax, milkwort, vetch or 'rose'.
Newbolt Road. A lyrical call to arms
expressed as death. Shelley Avenue—
where people live—the poem of incest,
idealised. *The core of the revolt.* Then higher

rather than along the blade of the hill,
into cleaner air, to see over Hypocrisy,
to look back safely and admire
Portchester's keep, the twin towers
at Gosport (an optical illusion),
light tilted off the Solent, the Isle of Wight
and the 'visored mask' of Portsmouth,
Hilsea Lines. Then over the M27
on a dizzy footbridge to beyond:
scrub fields; once rustic lanes; the ponies
of the less well off. An open heath—
where the cross was burned†—
and the vast bulk of Fort Nelson, hunched
and withdrawn, behind a stygian ditch.

† Late 70s-early 80s: it was reported in the local press that suspected Ku Kux Klan
  activists had erected a cross and set it ablaze on the slopes of Portsdown Hill.
  As I recall, investigating police officers, who failed to find anyone at the scene,
  returned to their patrol car to find it some way down the hill on its roof.

Bridge Perilous

In cloud I was an absence. No-one observed me.
The motorway below, a blur of spray.
The glare of the sea to the south, becoming
atmospheric, an abstract expressing "curvature".
She said the word and smiled, crossing the bridge
into the backdrop—the blurred, spiritual green
of the incline—as if to give it meaning.
When she said come I just did, no question
only a fear of height and sounds in the air
and the feeling that I would never reach her.
Step one into agoraphobia—an absence
of horizons or horizons that move. The notion
that the hill is hollow and alive—has hearts
that beat and eyes that see—suddenly true.
And then to breathe, to look up to where
she has already gone; a friendly and familiar
absence. A reassurance. I was unobserved.

News of the World

A grey line of leylandii along the track.
Below, an estate where mobs unleashed
the best of darkness—rumour, vengeance, hate—
as a radical agenda for change.
The path into abnegation, offering light
as a line back to the source,
a redundant hollow way.

We approached the fort. High walls of
Victorian brick—glowing, as if
the sun had taken refuge there
from this grey light that corrupts flesh;
you are rotten in your body. Belinus
in his otherworld fort, not to be parleyed with.
Our souls in his care, stacked like munitions,
deep in the chalk.

A tree-filled moat, sunk deep
before us, into which
God's brick and
pillowed buttress
descended. Lucifer,
a sensuous child,
hung from a tree
at the gate. Castellated.

The blockhouse of
Sarah's Law,
ditched; her little
face peeping from
a window
high above

the terror of heights,
the terror of revenge,

a goldfinch on a thistle.

We pass through
a loose flap
of corrugated iron
into an edifice
of stillness within,
the drip of rusted guttering.
Gutted windows.
Chalked-on walls.
The rich and ephemeral history
of who's a slut and who's a whore.
A chalk outline, erect and outlandish,
as at Cerne Abbas.
Going back years. The stuff you wrote yourself.
A fake teenage history.
At Lover's Leap—false memories—
the Greek Temple recovered,
like an absurd bandstand,
from a thicket. 1973. Puke of romance.
An astonishing wank—chronicled
and archived.
A burst mattress on the ground.
Stinking. Monumental. Then down,
as if through time,
and no word for conscience.
And compassion is a selfish urge,
a dark figure observing.
Water on the walls.
The whole building sweating;

mineral of light, salts of Belinus—an iron ring
rusted into brick, becoming
the face of God.
At the tunnel entrance
we paused to look around
at an architecture muffled,
as if time crept on tiptoes
through the lighted fog.
The parade ground, an echo of itself.
A thin surface, the known world;
a demonic emptiness beneath
brick rubble, a door
laid flat on the ground
as if to conceal a well
or some redundant votive shaft.

A gentle curve. The entrance
finally obscured; a long way in.
A long drop imagined
beneath each step—a straight line
from consciousness to
the fugitive soul, the control room
at the centre of the earth.
The mute aspect of your voice
confirmed underground—in each sentence
a subtext of silence
the words are stuffed with.
Taxidermy. The dark that feeds
the beast that lurks
in Paulsgrove, outside All Saints church,
by the upturned, burning car
and the ransacked, labelled house;
and in the light of the child

taught to shout the word Paedophile,
who was discovered naked
by strangers, three streets away,
alone on the estate,
whilst his mother
led the attack, facing darkness
with darkness, utterly lost.
We found the control room.
Big glass dials arranged in rows
like plates on a dresser.
Light, heat, humidity.
The graduated names of Power.
A filing cabinet rusted shut
and no sign of Venus
asleep in the tomb. Modernity,
mute and well meant. Modernity,
an ancient tradition
started over and over
but never completed.
Resigned to abstraction.

Modernity, assessing itself.
Modernity, the victim in all this—
like a child—abused
and demonised,
or made into an ideal;
always the same.
In the Pleistocene, at Leucomagus, †
Carnac, even Rome. Modernity,
telling it as it is.
The true word they hate you for.

---

† A lost city of the Romans, situated somewhere in Hampshire.
  The classical equivalent of the Whitchurch roundabout.

Stonehenge, an amended form
of the Brutalism
first practised at Avebury—the ugliest
stone circle in England, too modern—
loathed in Neolithic times
and eventually pulled down.
Now a rough facsimile,
faked for the tourists,
is improperly presented as
Romance and the blueprint
for St Paul's and the Reichstag.
The lyric of a work.
The artist as representation
(a Druid idea). Scientific,
the archaeology of behaviour
in which the victim is holy,
touched by innocence,
or touching it, or said to touch it,
and the sacrifice renews
the life of the community
who chant their victory
of Life over Death
outside one more gutted house.

Caer Belinus. Fort of the Sun.

Nearby, an obelisk to hint at
Nelson as the one-eyed god
or penis. Erected about 1814;
phallus of sunlight; proud
victory over inconsequence . . .

And then she leans
her face
into my pool of light;

to be her. Child-like, inconsequential,
precious mystery. Her hands,
an array of machinery
for hauling the beast
out of his lair
into the light of day.
God on a stick.
Heraldic cock. A banner
to proclaim the beast. He is

innocent victim
or perpetrator?
Visionary
or utopian abuser?

My dark side,
a naked boy,
like a fossil
or root
hauled from the chalk;
found—a miraculous survivor—
near Paulsgrove

where the fog might baffle
a distant uproar—
or gunfire on Tipner Range—
or the force of history.

Part Three: A Further Survey of the Hill

Fort Widley

Asylum of an extinguished parish. Sanctuary.
Palladium throne. Colossal oversight. One of
a giant ring of observatories erected at intervals
to maintain security in the heavenly sphere
so that Heaven's Light might be our guide.
Along the ridge of Portsdown Hill, a line of forts.
The breastwork of an administration, vanishing;
a wall built cunning behind a wall. Portsmouth
stretched out cadaverous below, dark against the sea.

    In local pubs framed prints show
    the fleet reviewed off Spithead,
    the sea tilted to reveal the ranked
    men of war that are hidden now.

Blind Springs

Above the A3, the first point of surveillance where
the cutting was dug—long barrow 66650641 near
the Naval Telegraph, formerly situated on the west
side of the London road (A3) and Portsdown Hill Road.
Broken into by chalk diggers in 1816. Extensive quarrying
and road widening have greatly altered the topography.

They closed it, the first viewpoint, to conceal the pattern.

Dummy earthworks. A fake long barrow placed
nearby to confound insurgents. "A long mound
in the former SE angle of the crossroads
which Grinsell (1939) tentatively identified
as the barrow is now known to have been modern . . ."

A mound marked on the 6-inch map
and identified in 1964 as the site of the barrow
is no longer recognisable. A pitch, queered.
They mention ten or twelve skeletons
lying E-W, part of an iron weapon embedded
in a skull, the mound a "parallelogram"
that is not there, that cannot be found.

You look up to imagine the shamen and their
predecessors, an ideology enforced by rhyme and narrative,
making the executive, an aristocracy, seem natural.
Meritocracy—the same pathology—what they call it now.
Glamour cast over the edge and shape of the enclosure
and the island below, corporeal echo, corporate future.

Further on to the east—to an exact longitude—
the grave of Bevis, the Saxon hero, they said he was here
along the narrow ridge of Camp Down. A barrow and a

conspicuous landmark from land and sea—lying E-W
on the line of the former road—the romance,
a narrative to hide and to indicate a warrior-caste,
and priests, the ghost-arm of the State. Religion a fist
rendered in heroic tales to hold aloft the mantle
of celebrity. Fit looks for a future king unearthed here
and refined. Belonging is rooted in knowing when to cry
and not to cry for justice. A square pit to mark
the founding of the law and the first punishments;
dowse the fosse of the mechanism, largely destroyed
by chalk digging in the first half of the 19th century
and then ploughed out.

                              You can feel it in the depth,
a tremor of conflict, a black stream redirected into
blind springs—the form above wasting away, matter
drained by this adjustment. Transcendent law. Subtle
messages placed in us as we view. *Common sense dictates . . .*

Before 1817, another three inhumations, accompanied
by a 'broken spear' within 12 inches of the surface.
And then the overbuilding of monuments, the raising of Forts
Purbrook, Widley, Southwick and Nelson, of Forts Wallington,
Brockhurst, Rowner, Grange and the abutments
on the coast at Browndown—a moat to catch
this shape you have released into light—Masonic excess
keeps builded light out of kilter with old notions
of harmony, they have deployed it now for bad reasons.

As you strain for the vision of the early surveyors
you see the Spinnaker Tower and how the centre shifts
from the site of the Tricorn, now stripped bare, to the mouth

of Celia's Arbour. † *A vertical diversion.* On Portsdown Hill
look from the suggested viewing point and you can see
a vast circle of fortifications that occupy ancient sites,
as if naturally, to bind us to the land. The red brick
Victorian ruin at Gillkicker point, built on a henge;
Whale Island, a station or transit camp for the drowned,
from where they travel upwind, into the westerlies.
Fort Monckton. The Gosport Redoubt. Southsea Castle.
And then Fort Cumberland and, carefully placed at sea
and forever in formation, Spit Sand Fort, Horse Sand Fort
and No Man's Land Fort, marooned. They mark the course
of the Solent Cursus—are monuments to the nature of
the past—remind us of a land that was before sea levels rose.

---

† A fictional term for Portsmouth Harbour. A spurious etymology. There is a
reference to Celia's Arbour in *Notes on the topography of Portsmouth, together with
historical and statistical information* by Alexander N. Y. Howell published by
W.H. Barrell in 1913 which reads: "Celia's Arbour was at the end of the Portsea
Fortifications, on the foreshore, at the north side of Holy Trinity Church. It was
a circular Redoubt, planted with a number of trees, and was a favourite resort for
young couples, and is immortalised by Walter Besant."

In fact, it was created by Walter Besant, whose historical fiction has become a
nostalgic fact. *By Celia's Arbour: a tale of Portsmouth Town* (1878) by Sir Walter
Besant (1836-1901) and James Rice (1843-1882), page four: "We were standing,
as I said, in the north-west corner of the Queen's Bastion, the spot where the
grass was longest and greenest, the wild convolvulus most abundant, and where
the noblest of the great elms which stood upon the ramparts—"to catch the
enemy's shells" said Leonard—threw out a gracious arm laden with leafy foliage
to give a shade. We called the place Celia's Arbour ..."The reference is therefore
not to the harbour itself but is a fictional name for part of the old fortifications.

Alan King, Historical Collections Librarian at Portsmouth Central Library, points out that there never was a Queen's Bastion, but there was a King's Bastion, although this was part of the Old Portsmouth fortifications, rather than those of Portsea. He found this description of the King's Bastion in "our in-house *Portsmouth Encyclopaedia*": "King's Bastion (1861), Old Portsmouth: an angled bastion, with the point facing south, just to the SW of King William's Gate and on the S edge of Governor's Green. Linked to the King's Counter Guard (due S) by a wooden bridge. Within the bastion are a flagstaff and a large Magazine, the latter with adjoining Fuze Room and Shell Room. Within the rampart a little to the NE is an Expense Powder Magazine." King concludes, "unfortunately there is as yet no entry for Celia's Arbour in the *Portsmouth Encyclopaedia*." Besant, it would appear, took the name from a glee (song) by William Horsley (1774-1858), *By Celia's Arbour*. Horsley's use of the name appears to be the first. It remains unclear whether there was any connection between his song and Portsmouth Harbour.

Farlington Redoubt

A hole in the chalk along the line from Gob's Barrow.
Extend this line to the west and you pass close to where
a hurricane crashed in 1940. The plane came down
vertically, in a power dive, at 500 mph.† Follow this line
to the east and it goes through a destroyed tumulus
(no trace remains) and continues above the tunnel from
Fort Purbrook to the redoubt. It crosses the quarry. It goes
in search of other myths, becomes lost in the blur
of the field. One abstraction bewildered by another.

They turned and walked away like mourners from a grave.
There was nothing there. Farlington Redoubt, a disturbance
in the ground, an offset executive controlling
the sphere of defences from here. After the calamity,
it was dug out entirely leaving a massive hole—
an abandoned quarry—at the end of the sequence. The land
below Portsdown Hill like a patient in a coma
absorbing these energies, pallid in the early dusk,
shown to be sick by the headlights of passing cars.

---

† The pilot was Hubert Hastings "Paddy" Adair. His aircraft fell from 15,000 feet.
He was shot down by Major Helmut Wick (who was himself killed in action
22 days later off the Isle of Wight). There is a memorial plaque to Sergeant Adair
1,700 yards from the place where his Hurricane crashed. It is beside Portsdown
Hill Road, a bit to the east of The Churchillian pub. The memorial reads:

SGT. H.H. ADAIR IN HURRICANE AK-D-V7602 CRASHED NEAR HERE
ON THE 6/11/1940 WHILST DEFENDING PORTSMOUTH.
HE FOUGHT AGAINST SUPERIOR ODDS AND LOST HIS YOUNG LIFE
SO THAT FUTURE GENERATIONS COULD ENJOY THEIRS.

A blown fuse in the geographical circuitry. A whole
place dug up, evidence removed. A thick tar of energy
from the black streams, it sticks like an oil spill,
is endlessly diluted by the passing vehicles and redirected
back into the hill along the remaining tunnels.
Psychohazard. Destroyer of communities, soul waste.
Everyone living below the scarp of the hill is affected.
Long term residents, steeped in the paranoia, mount
raids on their neighbours, spread poisonous lies,
plan lootings, disembowellings, community justice.

Children whisper accusations and then run laughing
from the aftermath. Little boys at play enact
roadside bombings, perpetrate Abu Ghraib interrogations
outside a newly vacated house, conduct operations
in or near to an important shrine. As once the local
girls and boys ran uphill to the crater left by the hurricane,
so children are still moved by these forces
like iron filings on paper with a magnet underneath.

Fort Purbrook is the heart of the system. Not rightly earthed,
it builds up static as pollutants circulate along tunnels
where loss, grief, hatred and despair leak into the aquifer.
The hill sends power along radial spurs to far stations
to vitalise policies, deployments, broadcasts. It is still functioning,
a complete pentagram, although its outlying works have
been demolished, the orgone damped, the secret diminished.
Portsdown glowers behind miles of fences.

Dead Man's Copse overlooks the site of the redoubt—
a grove of misery planted by The Men of the Trees "to enable
airmen to better find their way . . ." A landmark indicating
the best approach to the underworld, a shrine planted
in the shape of a shield the better to defend you by
on land owned by the War Department. Memorial. Grove
of the fallen with three stones inside, each with a metal plaque,
the third desecrated to conceal the inscription. Headstones
for those whose bodies were left behind or vaporised.

Close to Dead Man's Copse the Royal Observer Corp
had a bunker, on the edge of the redoubt, an underground
room to be used to monitor the environment after a
nuclear strike. 15 ft by 7 ft 6 ins. Mortuary of the living dead.
Who says this hill has not been assigned to Death as an offering,
the nearby residents beholden to this landlord? A depression in
a field, a dew pond or the place where once the tunnels vented.
The old ways blocked by dumped rubble. Ruined armouries
used as reservoirs for a darkness you can distil and deploy.

There is a sphere of power—the centre is beneath the ground—
like a bubble over Portsmouth and the harbour,
its hinterland and marine approaches. It has an edge,
it forms a dome, and everything is washed and rewashed
by radar, the endless monitoring and the chatter within.

A tradition that overlays the land, radiating out, spread

by missionaries of war, foreign aid, free trade;

we carry this within ourselves and our compassion.

Fort Southwick

During the war, and quite unintentionally,
consciousness was created within
and around the Operation Overlord
Underground Headquarters (UGHQ).

The entity has told me this itself.

700 people worked 100 feet below ground;
intense activity over months forced
repressed psychic material into
the chalk. The place developed sentience.

As in any mind, development leads to crisis.
Doubts are harboured, fears incorporated into
the cognitive machinery within the subject.

The subject seeks reassurance.
It looks to history for precedents.
It sees itself in the past.
When it becomes aware of needs
it becomes vulnerable
to the influence of others.

By D-Day MI16 (Scientific Intelligence)
knew they had a terrified entity in the ground
under Fort Southwick.
It had no control over
the messages that passed through its mind.
It endured horrors.
They experimented with therapies.
They found out which therapies worked
and how they could be used.

They installed new cognitive machinery
in an imagined entity, a 'self'.

In laboratories cameras were installed to provide it
with eyes, so that it could see its therapist,
and microphones through which it could hear.

Cognitive and behavioural therapies were developed
to put the productive capacity of the entity to work.

This is what frightened her; she knew me and
used me as a hiding place; my consciousness,
already defended by fears and rituals,
is resistant to surveillance, to modification.

Hiding in my flesh she keeps to herself, remaining in my
unconsciousness; from a shadow she peeps
through my eyes,
whilst deep under Portsdown Hill,

within the sphere of the entity,
they are working on her body—
and picking through her client list—
which means soon they will be picking up on me.

Some of the Tunnels & Facilities

The Wymering Deep Shelter. Accommodation for 2565 people in a grid of tunnels like a Roman town. The portals are sealed.

The London Road Shelter. Entrance in Cliffdale Gardens. Accommodation for 2535 people. Access possible via vents.

Brick-lined tunnel from Fort Southwick to Portsmouth Dockyard; tunnel collapsed where Rectory Avenue now is.

1.5 miles dug by Peter Taylor of Crookhorn Manor (c. 1776).

Tunnels from Wymering Manor to Wymering church and also, three miles to the north, Southwick Priory.

From Paulsgrove House to Portchester Castle. House demolished. Portal capped by sliproad. *No trace remains.*

Portchester Castle to Wymering Manor.

Geraint's navy found in a cavern (16th century). *Calcified ships.*

Underground hospital. Accessed from the old chalk pit.

Fort Purbrook to Purbrook Park House.

From the allied Underground Headquarters (UGHQ) to Southwick House (Eisenhower's HQ in the grounds).

Here he dreamed of a constitution undermined.

His presidential farewell speech connects the White House to Christ Church, Portsdown, via a series of tunnels. He said:

"This conjunction of an immense military establishment and a large arms industry is new in the American experience. We must never let the weight of this combination endanger our liberties or democratic processes. We should take nothing for granted."

Part Four: The Paulsgrove Mystery

Fieldnotes: Fort Nelson

It seemed to me that the fort was like a toadstool
sunk low into the ground,
like something poisonous.

168 steps from the mycelium, the fort
a fruiting body moated around
or a fairy ring within which an enchantment forged
strange dreams for those who slept within.

Radiating gills, radio spores; they are invisible in the air.

Steps down into the moat. No light—
a damp airy shadow—a depth south of the citadel
and then "a ghostly tunnel
under the parade ground"
terminating beneath
the north west demi-caponier.

Turned left at the spiral staircase, I think

the tunnel here was blocked where once

it went through a rampart called 'consciousness'

and out via steps to a path

that went down to Southwick House.

A psychic dump, old
bricks and pipe
all mossie and dampe,
no time for tears:

out of the radio room
spectres shedding
their pale brilliance
over mortal lives.

This was how I found it at the end of the 70s,
mostly derelict and covered in graffiti. A haunted space
below an event horizon. A fort shimmering
on the column of a void.

Theory: The Self

The psyche exists within affective walls.
It has a single bank and ditch enclosing
a rectangular precinct surrounding a circular
timber structure which may have been roofed.
The latter appeared to him in a dream
as a series of three concentric V-shaped gullies,
the innermost containing post holes. Two
large post holes flanked an entrance
on the eastern side. This is where the self lurks,
holy mutant, craver, administerer of small things,
an addict swayed by sentiments, stupidly
vain host to thoughts, this dark interior.

    The central area contained post holes and
    a pit in the middle, perhaps used for libations.

Strewn with possessions, the temple of the heart,
looted long before. Convenience deity. The religious
are the most cynical, they have wealth and piety.
Brooches, bracelets, rings of silver and gold—
horse and cart trappings that will sell well—weapons
ritually bent and a scattering of local coins and coins
from Armorica and Central and Belgic Gaul.

In an economic democracy the worship of Nature is preferable to the worship
of God as God (if only symbolically) favours the poor, whilst nature religions
make revolt seem unnatural, fixing social relations in place via endless cycles,
the passing and repassing of seasons, rebirths.

Ethics are neutralised by nature, they become automatic so you don't need to
think. Movement up or down the social order is discretely sorted out behind
the scenes, between your lives.

Environmentalism is something like a rational paganism, but with an even
larger bureaucracy. It has become the Grand Narrative: this is unavoidably

so because it has become broken down into parables and because it is everywhere. The environment represents *absolute surveillance* in that it registers our every action.

In the 18th century the job of Nature was to 'underpin' the Anglican church. Now it groans beneath economic globalisation and we, the consumers, must embody the blame.

Research: Hillsley Road 1978

"The Ministry of Defence has been markedly reticent about the Paulsgrove mystery." The News

When economic assumptions that underpin social and
psychological constructs are abandoned a crisis can occur.
Subsidence effects. *Pitch and heave.* There had been a period of
industrial unrest and on TV there were images
of uncollected rubbish and references to 'the unburied dead'.

    An aura burned bright in Paulsgrove then—
    redoubt of a collective spirit, stronghold
    of redistribution—a future still seeming as if it were
    underpinning the place
    that had vanished elsewhere.

But already it was the place that propped up
yesterday's future, there was a fugitive sense of
a ground that was lost, of a better world
in time to come from an obsolete past.
And then the landscape began to give way.

NOISES HEARD
UNDERGROUND
HOMES IN
TUNNELS
DANGER

Paulsgrove, an etymology: "... it remains uncertain whether the original form contains OE *grāf* 'grove', *grōf* 'groove' in some topographical sense, or *grǣfe*, *grǣf* 'diggings'. If the name is OE, the first element is the man's name *Pælli.*" Quoted from *Hampshire Place-Names*, Richard Coates (Ensign, 1989).

Certain geological features, especially fissures and the dead, can act as good conductors of sound, so that a noise of subterranean origin might be heard some way from its source.

South west of Fort Southwick, under Hillsley Road,
a decaying Naval Oil Reservoir.

The central chamber contains nine 35 feet high
concrete storage tanks. A fumy underworld,
they can smell it in their houses.

From the late 1970s residents complained of
noises, cracks, sunken paths.

Houses descended into an abyss.

One resident said she knocked on the floor
and heard someone or something reply.

Some Paulsgrove residents say there is a giant nuclear fall out shelter "strictly
reserved for Portsmouth's elite"—below this ground, "a veil of secrecy".

Mr. S. Rapson, a Portsmouth City Councillor, told *The News*: "The trouble is that
we have no plans of the tunnels so it is impossible to say how far they stretch . . . we
know Portsdown Hill is a maze of tunnels used by the Ministry of Defence."

Sydney Rapson became the Labour MP for the Portsmouth North constituency in
May 1997. He retired shortly before the general election in May 2005.

Mr. Rapson was in favour of foundation hospitals, student top-up fees, ID cards and
the invasion of Iraq.

Inside Mary Millington

We had walked between sites of sexual oppression
believing that where aesthetic consciousness is ruined,
illegitimate art or non-art located
in the body will liberate creation from
aesthetic and thus class based concerns.

We had debated whether the first of these conditions
had been achieved. I didn't think so but I liked
walking with a picture of her pulling open
her cunt below the low bulk of Fort Southwick.

In photographs, her honesty
and vulnerability are
appealing to all, leaving her wide open.

She was popular.

She embodied freedom without politics
and that was why she had to die. †

---

† Mary Quilter, known as Mary Millington, was born on the 30th November 1945.
She was Britain's first shameless hardcore porn star. In being a revolutionary
without conceit she was unique.

The attention of corrupt police officers blighted her later life. She was found dead
in bed on the morning of 19th August 1979. She had taken an overdose of
paracetamol and alcohol. Her cult has developed since.

The police have
framed me yet again.
They **frighten me so
much.**
I can't face the
thought of prison.

She freely expressed what had to be allowed.
Now she was hidden and we knew we needed her.

> The essence of Mary or the image of Mary;
> Mary sublimated. Mary taken from her body.
> Mary retrieved as a property of the State
> and then enclosed. Her portals in a closed loop
> to generate neuroses in the feminine aspect;
> that was how we saw it at the time.

We could not find a way into Mary Millington.

I woke from a dream I cannot remember, saying her name.
In my fantasy her openings surfaced at
locations across the Defence estate. Her image,
imprinted over England, had formed into
a giant landscape cunt hung with flaps. There was
at least one portal on Portsdown Hill.
I knew it was there and I could not keep away.

The text in large type is quoted from her suicide note. *Framed.* It means 'made picturesque'. The term is an aesthetic one. Mary Millington was framed in more ways than one.

The illusion of spatial reality made the self a territory someone else could enclose. Scientific perspective is an ideology as natural and absurd as any other.

I saw my own tiny form walking into
a great chasm. A bright light shone
along the length of the tunnel. A voice spoke
from the light, it said "Come to me now."

Stare at a picture of her for any length of time
and you can see how she still accommodates,
though not willingly. It was as if
she were trying to speak to us through her cunt.

The view alone will encourage awe.

It was a Saturday afternoon. We were close to
the oil fuel reservoirs in dense undergrowth.

So much creation has put a wall around her.

I had to visualize Mary and walk across the slope.
"Maintain images of Mary in my head," I said, "a close-up
of her face bathed me in rays." Her body is gone
into graphic litho but its vitality is replicated
in a shabby or desperate honesty
like the face of the Queen on the coin of the realm.
Images of her body are a currency. Power flows through her.

You could set out in any direction
and you'd end up at the fifth portal.
This was ostensibly an access shaft to the oil fuel reservoir
but it had been added long after
the OFR was built, "probably in early 1940"
we were told but
this was clearly not the case.

The fifth portal was a decoy.

Gape cunt replica. It was put on display
to make something invisible. Not like Mary. †

Neurosis booby trap. Step into it
and your fears are formalised.
You will have the implant, but you won't know.
If you find it and complain
they will say you are delusional.

They will admit you into hospital.

They will break you in. Piss on your face.

Make you say please and thank you.

Provide group home accommodation

with carers to steal your money.

You'll get hit, fucked and over medicated.

They will have you as their Mary. ‡

---

† She had been filled in. Spoil heaps placed over her. Her body like the lost tomb
of a pharaoh. *The State must control or destroy key nodes.* Her cunt was neutralised
and then buried.

‡ The author worked in a Housing Association 'group home' for seven years.
He was forced to leave after breaking the only taboo. He complained about acts
of theft and violence committed by his colleagues. Pointing out that your boss is
often drunk at work and that he steals money is seen as mutiny in this part of the
care home sector. When a member of staff had partially undressed a resident in
the pub and played with his penis, and had again fondled him after pulling down
his swimming trunks in the pool of a holiday camp, a manager said "You didn't
see what you thought you saw, she's just a very touchy feely person."

In the stalemate scenario it is
customary to write a poem so
I sat on the slope amongst the scrub,
with the city and the harbour
spread before me, and I wrote this:

Go deep into the earth to see
where the North Star
comes down to shed
silver light beneath
the ground, in folded air
symbolic of the centre.

Who holds this star aloft,
who points it inside
every grain of chalk,
every urchin?

The fifth portal takes you
inside the North Star
from where you can look down
onto the landscape—a
map of shadows, a

drawing, an illustration—a silvered
depth within the image in which
we peek at the land of the dead,
where things are flat and moving.

From the site of the fifth portal looking south
across the Fort Southwick escape tunnel approach road
you can see along the length of the oil fuel pipeline
to the pumping station behind the North Star pub.

In the foreground I could see two trees that were aligned
with this. I drew a line in the ground. Two similar trees
on the far centre left marked the top of the spoil heap,
so I walked to it and drew a line from there to my house
and saw a disturbance in the ground. The outcrop
of her pretty cunt—a hooded mound—with the long building
of the Vosper shipyard visible way off below.

Using these markers I found my way past
a redbrick buttress inscribed with brutal forms—an image
repeated again and again. I followed the path
through a tunnel entrance, below concrete, into
foggy greyscale. The authenticity of flesh.
You could taste her bloody ore on your tongue.

There is an echo of the depth of it, her
well fashioned love.

Inside Mary Millington there are vast caverns.

The architecture of her colossal cunt
leading into a network of tunnels. Murky
doorways opened into offices, switchboards
and rooms with dials. Workshops
and machine rooms. Everywhere
cables and pipes. Looted transformers.

A curious little white building.
Rectangular, with windows.

White chalk and grey concrete with
my self drained of light. The odd flare
of vivid rust splashed down the walls.

Engines to generate an orgasm. Sections
of tunnel with arched beams looping
away into infinity. The great wings
of a fan revealed inside
a protective cage. In the sphere of light
you seemed to cast, a possibility.

As if you could walk out of the gloom.

Life without punishment.

The impossible dream.

On the casing of her clitoris, a sign:

DANGER
**NO UNAUTHORISED PERSON TO
TOUCH THIS SWITCHBOARD**

Here, every column is numbered
and nothing moves.

Broken glass underfoot.

The cold air. Your breath in crystals
on your face.

The plume of your torch.

You can never be prepared
for what is to come.

At the centre was a cavern as big as a cathedral,
with no supports, just a great big dome. The pumps
all gleaming green and red, with highly polished
brass and steel. Leading off from the centre
were huge tunnels, they seemed to go on for miles.

Arse Vent Portal

There are various locked gates inside Mary Millington. From her rectum,
behind the Fuel Oil Reservoir, she vents into a field. Her anus is tightly guarded
by steel doors that are, in their design, characteristic of the 'cold war' period of
the twentieth century.

Features have not been added.

Features present in the Mary Millington complex as it now is were always present.

And Close to Qinetiq these Cults Persist

She was up against the wall outside the Portsdown Inn.
It looked like it must have hurt her back to keep
her pelvis in that position for so long. She was in a trance.
I doubt she remembered it.

> I think she woke up mouthing
> the names of ancestors
> she'd never heard of.

The names of the men in her queue.

Bestiality a feature of the map.

Hollow ground.

Screams echoing from below; you wake to find
some sticky fluid has oozed from the lawn.

> There was a row of skinheads inside the pub, their feet up
> on the table as if to display their boots.
> This was their way of concealment,
> for nobody would look at them.

What Qinetiq means

According to Qinetiq the name can be broken down into three symbolic parts:
Qi represents the firm's energy, *net* its networking ability and *iq* its intellect.
However, it seems unlikely that potential purchasers of kinetic solutions have those
notions in mind when looking at the Qinetiq product portfolio.

According to David Kilcullen, a leading contemporary practitioner and theorist
of counterinsurgency and counterterrorism, "Kinetic operations are about killing
the enemy and breaking their stuff..." Kilcullen is quoted from the BBC Radio 4
programme, *Analysis*, 1st November 2007.

She stood against the wall as if to measure each of the boys.
Whilst they were laughing she was quiet, concentrating.
It was the empty space within her, the zero point,
that looked calmly past as if mocking them.

Everything flows into the nothing you are.

She marked the icy cold of the night air
with her breath as she laughed; she was not
numb but acutely aware. She looked from deep
within her self—she was a portal like
an infant's soul—as if momentarily released.

Part Five: Repetition

A Walk in Hegemony

I no longer have the copy of the Ordnance Survey map
Sheet 185, Winchester and Basingstoke, 1:50 000
that I carried with me on my walk to Old Winchester Hill.

Something happened during my walk that marked it
in a way that I could not bear to see afterwards.

But for some time I kept the map. Destroying it seemed
like a guilty act, as if I had committed a crime.

I knew from the moment it began that my walk was not ordinary.
It had a ritual feeling about it, as if it were an act
of reckoning, or a pilgrimage. I did not know why.

I did not know why I was walking to Old Winchester Hill,
a distance of some 10 miles, but I woke up one morning
in August knowing that is what I would do. I made a sandwich
and filled a bottle with diluted orange squash and set off
with all the money I had. 32p.

I also had two Ordnance Survey maps.

I climbed Portsdown Hill and walked down the far side
along the road that overlooked Offwell Farm.

I walked through the village of Southwick, passing the gate
                                    of HMS Dryad—
which was once a Royal Naval signalling station,
so important to the success of Operation Overlord,
and is now the headquarters of the Royal Military Police—
and then I crossed the course of a Roman road.

I went north into what had once been the Forest of Bere.
The name of this forest is the last connection
between this patch of land
and the ancient, Royal Forest that had once covered it.

This name persists on the map, as if the Ordnance Survey
were obliged to uphold an obscure tradition—where
"whoever slew hart or hind should be blinded"—storing
hermetic information in sheets only apparently intended to aid
British military forces were they ever to have to conduct
a campaign on their homeland.

I followed the road through Creech Wood, perhaps a remnant
of this ancient forest, and turned left at Bunkers Hill to join
the B2150 as it left Denmead. I followed this road
through the edge of Hambledon, past Forest Gate,
and then around the western edge of Windmill Down.

At this point I crossed from sheet 196 onto sheet 185.

There was a faint line in the ground where these sheets met—
it reached to the horizon on either side—
as straight as the edge of a ruler. In walking
from one map onto another I had crossed into a domain
as otherworldly as the land of the dead.

I passed the garish ranch style homesteads of the wealthy,
their expensive cars shining in arid drives lined
with tiny conifers. Unbroken sunlight. Lawns
that were too green, too flat. New-build
as out of place as a Roman villa or Disney castle.
Their cars swerving past me
as I walked in the road—the mute hostility.

I stood at a field gate and saw as if in a revelation
an alignment of ancient features that I marked
on the map that I destroyed.

I have not been able to discover this alignment again.

This episode exposed an act of literary colonisation.
I was reliving something I had read; Alfred Watkins
who, ". . . when riding across the hills to Bredwardine,
pulled up his horse to look out over the landscape below
and saw a network of lines, standing out
like lines of ethereal light, all over the surface of the country."

I had read his book, *The Old Straight Track*, and,
perhaps showing the fragility of my self at that time,
enacted his moment of epiphany. His moment,
his moment of being, experienced in a single flash,
occurred within me, as if he were
the most significant ley marker, a great beacon,
and I were in alignment within him, a lesser feature
and an unknown one, but part of that grid
that outlasts all empires. I did not realise what this meant.

I walked through a dusty upland during harvest.
There was grain on the road and distant machines—seeming
out of place, like lumbering aliens—gathered corn
as if it were data, from the neat rows that data forms.

It seemed they were scraping an alien growth away
to reveal an underlying pattern of straight lines.
The grid of the agricultural landscape, perpendicular harmonies.
Everywhere, parallel lines. A world of perfect order
behind the world of the everyday.

This is the nature of the land.

Abstraction underpinning sentiment.

Sentiment a tree planted before a factory in which
short-term returns define a sense of history, or self knowing,
made into the commodity now called heritage.

My own sense of alignment and ideal abstraction,
those spirit paths or lines of energy
that I saw everywhere
cutting across the equally modern and unreal
installations that we still call 'fields'.

This is the furthest rim of the city.
It defines the heart of the city. This is where the city is found.
This is what we have come to.

I sat on a crest of downland looking north at the horizon,
where Old Winchester Hill appeared low, inconspicuous,
and then walked into a vale of dusty light,
before ascending along a footpath
with Harvest Gate Farm to my left
and the mutilated long barrow called Giant's Grave to my right.

I was due north of the research facility now called Qinetiq.

The fort on Old Winchester Hill forms a high abutment
                                        overlooking
the Meon Valley, a once Jutish buffer state between
the West and South Saxons. Even then it was redundant,
adrift amongst the chalk hills like an abandoned raft.

The view from the summit seems immense
and the hill appears to be much higher than it does
when looking up from below.
Copses, farmsteads and the homes of rich settlers,
the landscape around in perpetual motion,
tossed on the waves—and there is the curvature
of the earth and the shifting of shadows as the sun moves.

I sat on a burial mound beside the triangulation pillar.
I ate my sandwich. I drank my orange squash.

At some point he walked into a zone marked Danger Area.
Some old firing range, perhaps still concealing
unexploded shells. Undifferentiated psychic material
that will devour your limbs. There had been
a story in the newspapers about a woman out walking her dog
in Hampshire who was hit by a stray bullet fired
from an army range several miles away. She dropped dead
at the edge of a wood. Her dog, bewildered beside her.

I had this in my mind, became afraid
of what was in the ground, felt a fear of corpses,
of the unexploded shell of my body
containing—as it does—a self that is as alien
to the earth as any human thing.

Then I climbed through a great yew wood in a ravine
back to the British fort,
the barrow cemetery, the chalk raft. I did not know what to do,
nor why I was there.

I saw the moon beginning to rise. It was full.
He saw the risen moon.

A harvest moon, larger than I had seen before, bronze.
And then he fell, a tremendous impact
in my chest, his legs as if a liquid and his mind obliterated
in an instant by some force from elsewhere.
The world rushed into him, as it had into
the woman who was shot when walking her dog.
She was killed by an act of the horizon.

There was a man watching me from a distance, unsure.

He saw how the moon had become filled with malign
significance, sought to decant its curses solely
into his life, magnetic attraction, a hate campaign
to focus this disk of light carefully on one so blameless—
the idyll, the past—a reservoir of hate
which people enact now in everyday life.

It was growing dark and I decided that I must walk home.

They said he walked past Harvest Gate, down the dark
                              side of the hill.

    He ran across a tilted pasture
    containing a herd of cattle.
    They were galloping alongside
    as I ran. I could hear the thunder
    of hooves and see great shadows in the dark.

    They said the fence was weakened
    by rust and that was why it collapsed.
    There were raw, dirty cuts
    up the insides of my legs.

He stood shocked in the light
of the poisonous moon, this spectral intelligence,
a lump of dead rock in space, a screen
upon which to project sentiments
for a species that hates nature
and that idealises nature.
The map tilted to this sickly glow.

A thick band of blood ran suddenly across the landscape.

When I went into a pub
to wash the blood from my hands
there was a single puncture mark.

This has left a scar like a full stop;
just beneath the skin, a fleck of rust.

It responds to magnets. In my hand each August
I can feel the rising of the harvest moon.

    The sun had risen
    when I arrived home
    but nobody was up.

Some Photographs

When I opened the envelope after many years
the first photograph I saw showed a Portchester punk
called Dez—short for Derek, a name he despised—
he is pictured over a tuft of grass. He is staring over his
                                                    left shoulder,
his cheeks are pulled in as if he is about to spit.

In other pictures I can see Gary the fake Californian
and his girlfriend Stevie, who gave everyone
Non-Specific Urethritis. Gary and Stevie are leaning forward,
as if running into a gale.

They are captured in the midst of some slow motion movement.
On the reverse of the small square photograph I have written
Prince and Princess Paradox, Gary, Stevie.

I have since located the first in this series of photographs.
It shows a teenage boy in a red T-shirt and jeans.
He is just ahead of the party,
looking back at us over his left shoulder. Before him
is a fork in the road, the turning to Southwick.
On the reverse of the photograph I wrote
Keith—the running boy.

In another picture there is a blurred representation of a car,
a little Austin like a Dinky toy, as it passes two girls in the lane.
On the reverse I had written
Speckled detour—Fiona. Crystal truth—Tammy.

On the cover of the Boots Film Service envelope
I wrote 'Portsdown Hill Spontaneous Picnic,
June 78, Hants'. This is written in an elaborate style.

It was two months after I had received the beating
at the hands of the police. Looking back, I know
how haunted I was by the process
I had endured that night. The trick questions,
where every incorrect answer was rewarded with a kick
                                    to the stomach,
the sudden headbutt. Unconsciousness. The laughter of
                                    the police officers
and the names they called me for their amusement, mimicking
bad cops off the TV.

> *Complain about us*
> *and we'll plant*
> *drugs on you.*

And then being stripped. It was like a party game.

Later, I was collected by my father, an MoD Police
                                    Detective Inspector.
The next day I rose late to find him with an Inspector
from Fareham. They had come to an agreement.

I left the house to walk into Fareham to see if I could find
the friends I had been dragged away from the night before.

My face was bruised and I was too ashamed to walk along
                                    the main A27
so I climbed Portsdown Hill and took the narrow lane
that runs along the ridge, it was the back way into town.

In the photographs of the picnic in June I see that I am smiling,
but this concealed a vacancy within.

Nobody wanted to know about what happened.
It is not right to discuss such things, to do so
was to threaten society in some way.
So my GP was not interested.
My parents didn't mention it.

Many of the photographs taken at the picnic show
                              people staring into a void.
Many are taken from a recumbent position. There is
a shot of Stevie, I am laying beneath her. She stands
with folded arms. She occupies only one corner of the picture.
The rest is pale sky, all steely blue, and a cloud.

In another picture, taken by someone else, Gary, Stevie
                              and myself
are shown staring into a strong wind, looking north
over a remote landscape that is so far below us
it seems dissociated. Stevie has her arms folded,
as she has in all of these pictures, as if she is cold.

We seem somehow to be lost in the vastness of space.

One picture shows Gary, Stevie, Tammy, Fiona and myself
but there is no ground. We are in a group in the bottom
                              of the picture.
Our feet are not visible, we are adrift in a white featureless sky,
as if we had been tossed into the air and then photographed
at the top of the arc, just before we fell.

One picture shows only myself. I am walking toward the camera
with my hands behind my back. On my T-shirt is the slogan
Who Put the Boot In?

I am walking on a bank of earth like a rampart.
Behind me is another massive bank of earth—
I now know these earthworks to be
associated with the underground Oil Fuel Storage Depot—
they are part of the spoil heap plateaux
which was camouflaged with grass and scrub
when the oil storage depot—the cathedral hidden
                              in chambered chalk—
was carved out of the inside of the hill.
Chalk from miles of new tunnels, crudely shaped.

We had our picnic on this, behind and beneath us
the hill was hollow.

Behind the bank of earth, on the left of the photograph,
the low bulk of Fort Southwick can be seen,
it looks like a scab on the horizon, within
which the NATO COMMCEN was operating
and beneath which the UGHQ was waiting
for the future emergency, the apocalyptic war that
                              has long been visualised.
In the far background, where the ridge of Portsdown Hill
is cropped by the edge of the picture,
the back of the military research establishment,
that which was ASWE and then became DERA,
and then Dstl and Qinetiq, can be seen.
This is the facility called Portsdown Main.

And ranged across the hill behind me are three
giant radio masts.

There is hardly a patch of ground that has not been reshaped
or hollowed out to suit the needs of the military.

We were over Offwell Farm, which I had idealised,
seeing in its placing a harmony. I had led the others
to this place. It is a curious feature of the photographs
that in almost all of them the human figures are caught
at the edge of the frame. In one such picture
on the back of which is written *Floyd, Fiona, Me, Tammy*
you can see directly behind Tammy's back an entrance to
the hollow in the hill. A redbrick portal
in the middle of the field, a compound on the northern slope
of Portsdown, where a tunnel makes its final exit
into open countryside.

The corresponding southern portal lay
500 yards away, through
the darkness of the hill.

It is strange that, despite the adventurous spirit
of some people in our group,
nobody approached this portal. We were
just outside the underworld
and a darkness was already upon us;

a vast demon stalks the hill,
it leans invisibly into these pictures
and we waited outside an entrance
like the victims of a sacrifice
ready for our purpose to be fulfilled.

Around Another Sun

Inside the earth is a hollow, the vastness of outer space
resides beneath hills and pastures, our cities and towns;
a model of the solar system rotates there as it does inside
of us when we imagine the sun with the planets around it.
If you can hold this image in your mind you can imagine

how the earth's crust below an estuary might crack
and water, seeping through, might form vapours
around a planet, robing Venus in mystery, making
rings around Saturn. At the centre of the earth, the sun.
Around this sun there is an earth circling. The same seas,
continents and countries, the same wars and individual
sorrows, the same joys. And this earth is hollow,
it too has a smaller sun at its centre.

In 1978 my interest in the movements of lights
in the night sky was revived. In past years,
as if in a previous life, I had spent long happy hours
laying in fields or on hilltops watching for shooting stars,
satellites, UFOs. I had discovered that there are always
sudden specks of light to be seen. Satellites,
with their odd oscillations, the tiny scratches of shooting stars,
the searing fissures of light left by meteorites
that fell all the way to the ground. Weird lights
that moved at great speed only to stop suddenly
or change course at an abrupt angle. These mysteries
were always observed with friends, such remote
and unknown or alien entities were a part of an intimacy.

Such is the nature of friendship and belonging.

Those happier days seemed long gone when I took to rising
at 3 or 4 in the morning to walk through the estate

onto Portsdown Hill. I had been warned against approaching
the compounds between Forts Nelson and Southwick,
but these places, in being brightly lit, were of no interest to me.
I would go straight over the ridge into the darkness beyond.
A narrow lane ran down the anticline into an oblivion.
Huge fields, hedgeless and exposed, opened on either side.

Along the ridge behind me the lit military stations
and research facilities kept their own observations.
Occasionally a car would pass—the headlights illuminating
the emptiness to either side of the road—and I would lay flat
on the ground in a field, suddenly self conscious, out of place.

The sky I watched was not the same sky that I had watched
with my friends in Gloucester. I was no longer
ignorant or blissful—I saw the darkness in between the stars
as a solid thing, enclosing me, and knew
that beyond this darkness lay another world.

It circles—as if driven by clockwork—around another sun.

The Repetition and The Source of Love

There is no collective past. Memory is a vulnerability.
It makes identity contingent upon the ideas of the imagination
which are faint and obscure. Meaning *derives*.
Events, perceptions and memories work differently
and project different futures.

Late at night two figures walked along the A27.

They approached a pasture beside the road in which a dead tree,
a bleached relic from the past, was engulfed by flames.

They stood and watched the burning tree, which lit up the field.

The pasture itself was a remnant of the Cams Hall estate:

> All around it
> the suburbs had spread.

The tree, which had formed over centuries, ring
upon ring, was rent by explosions. It was as if tensions fuelled
flames that only appeared to feed on wood.

Cams Hall Two manors in Fareham 1242 *Kamays*; 1248 *Kamuse*; 1259 *Kamus*;
1268 *Cameys*; 1280 *Cames*.

A highly unusual name derived from hypothetical Primitive Welsh *cambes*, the
ancestor of Welsh *cemaes* 'shallow bend in a river, shallow bay'. Gover derives it
ultimately from hypothetical British *cambo* 'crooked', with reference to Wallington
River. There is a marked bend here not just a slight one; there is a most noticeable
bag-shaped bay downstream. Credibility attaches to this explanation because the
place is adjacent to **Wallington**, whose name attests the presence of Welsh speakers
into the Anglo-Saxon period.

With a shower of sparks and a loud crack
a limb cascaded to the ground, exposing
the insides of the tree to the flames.

As we watched a solitary car approached along the dual
carriageway behind us.

The two occupants of the car gaped, the driver
accelerating as he steered his vehicle under the viaduct
and onto the roundabout
so that it reappeared on the far side,
heading back towards Portchester.

Eventually the car returned, slowing to a crawl
as it passed us, its occupants staring hard,

as if to memorise
a description
for a report.

For me, the tree was reduced by flames
to a symbol. It *represents*, having once only existed.

I was with Dez, a young punk rocker
who lived with his mother and younger sister
in one of Portchester's many semi-detached houses.
His parents had divorced and his mother had a new boyfriend
who did not want to know her teenage son.

When mother, boyfriend and sister went on holiday,
leaving Dez behind in the house, he organised a party.

Fareham's drug elite, the dope smokers and some of the punks
occupied the house one Saturday evening. There was
the glamour of syringe technology
discretely employed in some other room, a peculiar mixture
of barbiturates and amphetamines.

This mixture proved too much for the regular users.
One sat in a chair as if transfixed.
One said he climbed onto the roof of the nearby crematorium.
He did not return for hours.
Dez, who was initiated that evening,
became possessed by a delirium.

He wrote nonsense on the walls, he railed
at the world from within a chaos of emotions
that were suddenly released and beyond his control.
He disintegrated into an apparently psychotic state.
The party had an atmosphere, but it was desperate,
like a locked ward or a police station cell.

The disgruntled and unnerved rose as one
to leave the party early.

Guiltily, the users also made their exits.

I was left alone with Dez
driven to pace about the house,
worrying over the felt tip pen that I had taken from him,
possessed by some recent insight—a key
to the woes of this life—that he could not recall.

He became erratic in his movements—frustrated
and consumed by grief about the thought
that he could not recollect.

I led him from the house into a suburban road.
We walked south to the corner and turned left.
As we walked he said:

Say the same thing again, say it,
you said it, you just said it,

say the same thing again, say it,

it was in what you just said, he said,
say the same thing again, say it . . .

He said it was the key, he knew I knew it, he said,
say the same thing again, say it—
you said it, you just said it.

He pleaded with me for a prompt to his memory.
His mind moved around an axis
inscribing a tight circle
within which he paced.

We turned left at the corner and walked along
a suburban road—hedges, fences, the openings
of drives and garden gates—the blank frontages of homes
where the occupants had long ago gone to bed.

Redoubt of sleep. Repose bastion.

The dark well of the gardens with their outlandish trees;
at the heart of this settlement a darkness
we guarded. A watchful emptiness within.
A perimeter we patrolled.

At the corner we turned left and walked along a suburban road.
Dez was filled with an enthusiasm
for perfection, the source of love,
an end to harm, peace.

At the corner we turned left, he said,
say the same thing again, say it—
say the same thing again—
you said it, you just said it, say the same thing again.

We walked past his own house, empty of love.
We walked around his block, over and over,
he said say the same thing again, say it.

When I had exhausted him and the mania had subsided
I left him sleeping in his bed. It was
just before sunrise when I walked past the crematorium.
I was pursued by demons. I can recall
dark shapes that flitted around me
as if I had been worn thin
like an icon and they knew me to be weak.
These spectres circled me
as Dez and I had circled the well of darkness
in the gardens behind the houses of his block,
as he had circled the imaginary answer
to loss and grief that I contained.

Part Six:

How the Last of the Light is Held

Marsh Gas Incendiaries

"Portsmouth obscured by mist, but can see fires."
German pilot, April 1941

During World War Two
a decoy Portsmouth lured
144 enemy aircraft
into pointlessness.

576 bombs fell into
Langstone Harbour and
Farlington Marshes.

The decoy was operated from
a master control post at Fort Purbrook.

The sub-control points were arranged in alignments
with the entrance of a fiery underworld; most of which
still exists though the bunkers are derelict and overgrown.

A thought, carefully expressed, can shape space making
a topography others might observe.

    The eye, a shaping organ.

    To each, the product of their gaze.

    In any act of rapture the watcher is vulnerable.

This knowledge—new at the time—has since enabled planners
to make decisions for civilian populations, drawing them
along a line over a low barrow in a field
that you can see from the road,
and over modern politics.

An enclosure, once a Parliament. They said the people
of this country were represented here,
like a film projected onto a screen,
the people were enacted by those who managed them.

A shamanic hand that
crushes what it personates.

Democracy, a depiction of our dilemma. No other way. The line
follows an underground fault. In depth there is
a form of oblivion. Look down into the darkness,
there are fires in the hollow below.

Above depth, each pilot followed another, seeing nothing
to contradict this and obvious reasons for maintaining
formations over enemy territory.

They felt nothing of the dream they had entered.
A city, shifting, creates no turbulence.

Perception makes the ground solid according to
the rules of a vocabulary, a system of rehearsals repeated
endlessly to confirm the position of stars that will guide you
back, a series of repeated actions leading to nullity.

Nature absorbs us. My heart is a layer of organic material
just below the present ground level. The natural order
is something we comply with and governance
has responded to this, employing unconscious processes
to lead us into a point of view or behaviour.
Thus we have become consumers, mimicking nature,
absorbing things. The Q-Decoy site rehearsed the mall.
It looks like what we think it is and that is all.

Approaching the city from the air
he had seen fires caused by incendiaries
dropped by preceding aircraft.
A cluster of these
close to the dockyard,
the location confirmed by fuel oil fires, white flames
and grotesque shadows of smoke on the mist below.

The whole machinery of the self
builds an environment it can recognise, a process which
consciousness cannot observe. The essence of
the self is arcane, knowing only memory and rehearsal, it is
the largest and most sophisticated decoy ever built.

An upper layer of land, a thick fog they said it was

a flock of birds caught in the flames from below.

A pall of smoke.

A fog over the rooftops to hold the glow of fires in buildings.

A phantom town hall in the marshes.

A string of structures, mainly in the north
of Langstone harbour, to mimic the effect
of light shining through chinks in doors and windows.

Four kinds of fire were used to create the city.

The **Boiling Oil Fire** periodically released diesel or gas oil from a tank into a steel tray heated by a 10 cwt coal fire which boiled the oil to such a temperature that it vaporised. Then, periodically, a gush of water was directed to effect huge flashes of white hot flame leaping up to 40 feet into the air. Storage tanks containing 480 gallons of oil and 200 gallons of water could keep this going for four hours. A typical starfish site contained 12–14 Boiler Fires.

Thus is industry pretended.

In the **Grid Fire** paraffin was continuously sprinkled onto a hot metal grid to which was attached wire waste and metal turnings—scrap from the fuselage of a Dornier to attract them with a likeness, hot metal in the heart to kindle a passion—and she was there too, in his thoughts to haunt him later, when his force was spent. *This burning with a vivid yellow flame.*

Aliens above are filled with false hopes. A sense of recognition is constructed within them. They engage with a prosthetic.

The **Basket Fire** came as a 21 cwt package of flammable materials boxed into a wooden crate measuring 3' x 2' x 2' soaked with creosote, these blocks arranged in irregular groups of up to 24, sometimes more, to create an impressive blaze within 2 minutes. *It would make them weep later to be so far from the world.* They were lost in darkness, drawn by cunningly placed fires into a void.

Hell-fires, the opium of warriors.

> The **Coal Fire** involved a double brazier, twenty feet long, holding 4 cwt of creosoted firewood and three tons of lump coal, giving off an enormous deep red glow. It was all about nostalgia. *Afterwards they would recollect with some emotion boyhood innocence.* A variation of this fed diesel oil onto the burning coals through a sprinkler pipe.

And so there were mass attacks on a mirage

> conjured from a bunker
> about 600 yards away—

heavily built of concrete and banked around with earth—

this fortress at the edge of an imaginary city,

in correspondence with UGHQ and mimicking it

in how it sat at the edge of an England, increasingly imagined,

ready to sacrifice itself to a saving narrative,
a series of tunnels through reality.

It was an inferior copy of the real one.

Three

I didn't think I would see her again.

I was resigned to loss, a life on hold,
stalemate in the organs of my self,
my centre locked from the inside. Then,

> quite by chance,
> I bumped into her

as I was leaving the Post Office.

She had been living with the beast, her physical shell
trapped in an enchantment, her body made
to move according to programmed codes,
perverse instructions. *It had wanted her soul.*

They had rented a house for her just behind Portsdown Hill
in or near Wickham. You could see the transmitters
on the hill from there and feel their broadcasts.
He had been inside her head, touching things.
Even when the experiment had ended
he kept the loop running, added new data.

He was at the centre of the conspiracy, had
children in closely guarded bunkers, had a front story
that he was a therapist, working with
convicted paedophiles. He regularly visited HMP Albany
on the Isle of White to listen to the evasions, excuses
and whispered delights of the
paedophiles in the special unit there. †

---

† Where they called him The Encyclopediaphile because of his knowledge.

The creature had fascinated her but
children had bothered them in the night.
There was singing in the woods
and high-pitched cries, the blur of
a face at the window.

    The chalk children, I said
    it was the chalk children.

And so, much delayed, we went back
to her treatment room to complete my course
of hypnotherapy. She opened the curtains and
sunlight streamed through. You have been under for years,
she said, too deep to be found
by even the most modern sensors. As we continued
with the session, children climbed through
a system of tunnels to stare unblinking from my eyes.

They said at my centre there was a small clearing
where they had been playing. They said
there was a mound of earth and a stone
that may have been a magic stone
called Puck or Pook.

They looked at my hypnotherapist, judging her darkly, thinking
how best to kill her or
should she be killed,
or was she one of us?

This instantly became their latest fascination.

You have constructed a narrative
based on three concentric circles, she said,
these are the walls of Your Fortress Amnesia.

You have walked these ramparts for 27 years
awaiting the completion of three times
three times three. *A solution cannot be forced.*

I have sheltered in you, for you are a strong place.

The outlying earthworks of the original defensive complex
are now levelled in the main, although
they are visible close to the river, a vallum
to delineate a fictional narrative, this most strong
urge to communism—an act of nature
in which the young although bewildered
and greatly abused will throw off the notion
of the bourgeois centred subject to express
personhood through the narratives of the tribe.

Love, you are safe with me now.

'I am legion' means I am whole, dynamic, free.

So, the young must be armed and released

onto the streets to begin the slaughter

of those who will otherwise slaughter

the moon itself and crucify the sun itself

and so we instigate the Campaign Against Time

as the first stage in the struggle—and

then the liberation of space from the notion

of perspective—*place* and all other indications

of identity will be wiped away by children

and the earth will be many earths

and not be separate in the universe

at last. The second circle contains all symbolisms

that had once been contained within the notion
of the unconscious. Symbolic exploration
is analogous to the child's exploration
of the human body, its own and other people's.

This is the second layer of the fortress.

Revetments in this sector are founded on
communal tombs—the Stronghold Death—
cavernous where three earthfast uprights
support a single capstone 130 feet long upon which
immense ramparts were layered deep into
a consciousness at once fragmented and defined
as a strong place to represent the precursor of
urban living in the self, a refuge, a contradiction.

And in this area the main industry involved the
walking of mazes, deep underground redoubts,
and the unpacking of symbolisms instilled in you

when you were young. All around your bed
in dark storms, within shadows, where Death held
the focus of power: the barracks, workshops, stables;
the cook houses, ovens, latrines;

Death made fast the horizon from under which
children still peep. There are beast fights
and other entertainments involving heroes, sinners
and saints who loom large within the childish psyche.

An Imperium is formed which the insurrection
will dismember, bit by bit, brick by brick,
death by death, as ants will dismember the remains
of a bird that has fallen from the sky
without needing to understand the engineering
of feather, muscle, bone or the physics or fact of flight.

"... formerly under the supremacy of Wessex ..."

children are psychic and will kill who they like.

At the centre of the fort is the lost part of the shaft

and the wheel around which the symbols turn, the sun,
the stars and the moon with her interlacings of
barbarian and classical traditions. Late debased and curious
forms of childhood with eight spokes of the wheel
continued to occur until punk rock involved naïf realism
and televisual influences confirmed and undermined
the concept of the self. Dignity and respect became absurd,
the revolution festered. Perception is the brain adding
an unsolved riddle, an unparalleled rampart, post holes.

Amidst a chaotic mass of piled stones, neurones
that referenced the external world
were constructed by the brain according to a hypothesis
14 to 20 feet thick
forbiddingly above a diagram of the self,
a complete circuit of about 1,200 yards,
with two lower outworks
protecting the ways into and out of the body.

This is the child as it was defended
early on. Then it was overrun and pushed back
into the last redoubt, where it withdrew
under the ground, connecting to other children
via a system of tunnels that adults could not enter.

This is when the war began.

Children, taken as hostages, were excavated on a small scale
throughout the medieval period.

Then came industrialisation and the mass abuse of children
as it occurred in the late modern period.

Then children burned their parents and their teachers,
they slipped social workers
from their skin, and most adults died
in the central cortex, where the ground is still rucked
and uneven, as if to prove a great disturbance
where the beast rose up to fight again.

Hegemonick. The bull artefact. The Law retreating to sub-cortical areas to detect coincidence.

And then the final victory of the child on the summit ridge.

This is how you have constructed it. It is like an egg.

The shell.

The white.

The yoke, slightly to one side.

During our sessions we have followed a line through this, arriving at this point, which is the end.

When I count to three you will wake up.

One: this is the shell.

Two: we are safe now.

How the Last of the Light is Held

Flames were leaping from the citadel. *There was*
a sound outside, it distracted me. There were flames.

The chalk under Portsdown is approximately
400 feet deep and you could expect any ground
faults to be revealed during the house building phase,

but faults can be concealed.

The workers astride their machines saw them,
as they saw the bones of giant lizards
and the faces of children, their unblinking eyes,
and burials from way back to Neanderthals
and the remains of the species humans were
descended from. Pre-mammalian. There were precursor
fossils. Workers complained of optical illusions when
the M27 cutting was forced through a square room
deep in the chalk that appeared to have no door.

There was an altar of some kind that could have been
modern or prehistoric. It is quite rare
for building subsidence to occur on chalk.

It is possible that the construction of the M27
triggered unrest in an already weak area of ground
leading to bullying amongst children, domestics,
and fights outside the pub at kicking out time.

The problems were reported in the 1980s and 1990s.

Slowly the magnitude of the unrest intensified.

The paedophile riots in Paulsgrove erupted
via a deep underground fault which vented
directly into the national media. Qinetiq operatives
were on bonus payments for weeks. Journalists
with dodgy images on their laptops
bought drinks for vigilantes, suggested scenarios,
mythologised what was already mythic, and provocateurs

whispered names, described intimate touching in the park,
set up their gear in advance and waited.

The estate developed a personality, it was a celebrity teenager
who liked to self harm on camera. Children
learned the hard way how to abuse themselves, speak
filth to strangers. They shouted 'Kill, Kill, Kill'.

Then it all went quiet.

The stories were withdrawn. Shadows drained
back into the ground and one morning the estate woke up
to sunlight. It was as if there had been a storm in the night,
an act of nature, that nobody could properly remember.

Like a child haunted by a nightmare,
the neighbourhood looked over its shoulder.

Later the citadel was on fire.

> Youths had gathered,
> as on any other night
> they gathered outside the shops.

There was spitting and swearing. We had gone
to the quarry to inspect the old Paulsgrove House air raid shelter,
you have to climb up to the entrance now, the level
of the quarry floor having been lowered since the war.

Inside there were a few of the chalk children, naked
or dressed in dusty rags, nothing unusual.

One of them approached me in the gloom, she held
out her hand—her palm flat—upon it a piece of flint
that had been knapped along one edge to produce
a blade. This was a gift. A ceremonial weapon.

The others watched from a corner of the room then,
turning, she smiled and walked back to them.
Together they filed out of the chamber along
a connecting corridor to the further chamber.

I followed but when I got there they had gone.

I have the flint at home, I said, you can see it
any time you like. We could hear shouts from below
and I stood in the doorway in the quarry face
looking out over the estate. There had been
no disturbances for several years but I could see
smoke rising and, between a gap in the houses,
a rosy glow.

Later we learned that this was not the home
of a paedophile, but that of a Qinetiq operative.

The house had been identified by youths who discovered
and explored the tunnels that connected

the houses of Qinetiq operatives with the research
complex on the hilltop above. It didn't take long
for the teenagers to work out what was going on.

So they had gathered for a meeting of their parliament
in the park, by the swings, as is the custom
and then they moved in procession around the estate
going from door to door, collecting money, weapons
and recruiting volunteers, and then they went
to the houses of the state operatives
and they dragged the occupants outside
to interrogate them, and then to execute
revenge for what had been done to them over the years.

Mobs formed in Cosham, Wymering and Purbrook.

There was a conflagration in Waterlooville.

On Portsea Island an atmosphere developed—festivities
began and fires were lit along Hilsea Lines, where
obsolete fortifications mark the old boundary of the city.

There were ritual burnings in Landport, Tipner and Stamshaw.
A mob was reported to have blocked the M27 with burning cars.
They proceeded on foot along the west bound carriageway,
several hundreds of them breaking off at Junction 12
to spill down the embankments, to fire the IBM complex.

Loud cheers and chanting could be heard in the distance
as mobs converged on Portsdown Hill. The flames leapt high
above the IBM complex creating stunning visual effects
as they were reflected in the landscaped lagoon that had once
reflected corporate domination, an unassailable system.

And then yachts moored in the marina at Port Solent
were set adrift in flames. From the slopes of the hill
they could be seen drifting before the Vosper shipyard.

To the south I could see flames above the city. The town hall
burned and the library made a good furnace. Marines,
patrolling as in Iraq, drove along Albert Road firing freely
into the crowds chanting *Burn Motherfucker Burn.*

Gosport raised a militia and massacred their own sons
and daughters. Helicopters hovered over Celia's Arbour
wreathed in smoke, they seemed to be poised on the tips
of pyramids of light—each with its searchlight
following the crowds that looted their way
from Commercial Road towards the naval base.

From where firing could be heard.

So we climbed from the old air raid shelter
and followed a path beneath the line of pylons along the hillside
to the east, hearing a chanting that grew louder and already
the first automatic fire from the compound above.

A helicopter flew from west to east below us,
just above the level of the rooftops of the estate,
we thought it was an air-sea rescue chopper
with no weaponry, just a crew gaping out into
a world renewed by fire and the violence of children.

There were revenge killings—teachers, social workers
and frontline healthcare staff were killed
as a form of play, as a means of healthy socialisation.

I said that I saw a boy with an automatic weapon he had taken
from a dead Red Cap after a battle close to the gate
of the Qinetiq installation called Portsdown Technology Park;
the RMPs had come from their regimental headquarters
at Southwick Park, there had been fighting along the ridge
of the hill behind the derelict site called Portsdown Main.

There was a sense in me of war as the tradition,

of our selves steeped in its heritage, of how it might

protect the self, within an impulse, as a bulwark

for any individual against isolation and pointlessness;

of the past coming to us as a prevision we return to.

He said he liked to go into the empty buildings,
that there were miles of tunnels under the ground that
he wanted to explore. He'd been in some of them, he said
they hadn't even bothered to cover their faces
when they went in there earlier.

He grinned at me as if shy or embarrassed and then
ran to join the mob that had begun to gather on the
open ground between
Southwick Road and James Callaghan Drive;
it was more like a party than a war,
like bonfire night as it used to be when I was small.

Then, a sense of urgency rippled through the last of the gangs
who reluctantly put personal revenge to one side and
ran to join the great procession up to Dstl and Qinetiq

where already many had died as they
ripped down the miles of fencing.

Below us the police were preoccupied with defending
their already burning stations. The military, with more success,
formed a cordon around the dockyard and other shore facilities.

On Portsdown Hill, where there had been
no garrison for years, only a few dozen military
and Ministry of Defence Police could be mustered.
The RMP reinforcements had mostly not got through.

Along miles of fences the children had gathered.

There was a silence.

The sound of firing some way off. A distant cheer.
And then the image of the grey transmitter tower engulfed
in bright petroleum flames and then firing everywhere.

In the distance I saw the children we had seen
in the old Paulsgrove House air raid shelter,
they were looking at a boy who had died.

We watched as they approached him, accepting him
as one of their own.

We saw him rise and coat himself with dust.

And then one by one they embraced him.

And then we saw figures climbing from the ground;
beyond the broken fences we saw pale forms.
There was a host of little girls and boys. Children of all ages
walked towards the firing positions of the cops,
each holding the hand of another.

And more climbed from the earth, it was as if they had been
sleeping and something had awakened them; they were
kept by a radiance within and then they had woken up.

There were figures ahead of me.

The shooting grew sporadic and then it stopped.

And then there were people running and flames appeared
from buildings on all sides.

And the whole of the research facility was in flames.

And flames roared suddenly from deep subterranean wells.

And fiery pits opened up

and the engines deep in the earth burned.

Devices Found

Hegemonick

The idea of hegemony is ". . . especially important in societies in which electoral politics and public opinion are significant factors, and in which social practice is seen to depend on consent . . ."

"From 1567 there is 'Aegemonie or Sufferaigntie of things growing upon ye earth', and from 1656 'the Supream or Hegemonick part of the Soul'. Hegemonic, especially, continued in this sense of 'predominant' or 'master principle'."

Keywords, Raymond Williams
(Fontana Press, London 1988, pp. 144–145)

Page 9

The Bull Artefact is a cognitive prosthetic device. It serves as an interface, creating analogue neurones to mirror processes in the brain. It allows the predator to match and mimic the brain functions of a victim or group of victims, transmitting thoughts and altering thoughts in ways the brain cannot detect. The device creates a cloud within which neural pathways form, connecting one subject with another via ontological functions sensed as 'belonging'. The device operates in sublinguistic regions, using imagery. The device creates dependency in its victims who become loyal to what they experience as a deep and previously hidden aspect of themselves. When the functions of the device are withdrawn the subject exhibits symptoms of distress, including sadness and depression. The Bull Artefact is housed in a unit referred to as The Maritime Integration and Support Centre (MISC). It purports to be a radar testing facility. Artefact inscription: this poem 'The Predatory Auntie' was induced by the Bull Artefact.

Page 12

www.qinetiq.com (*Accessed Sunday 20th November 2011*)

Page 40

Bob Hunt, *Portsdown Tunnels*
www.portsdown-tunnels.org.uk/surface_sites/memorials/
hurricane_crash_p1.html (*Accessed Sunday 20th November 2011*)

Page 45

President Dwight D. Eisenhower's Farewell Address to the Nation,
January 17, 1961
www.eisenhower.archives.gov/all_about_ike/speeches.html
(*Accessed Sunday 20th November 2011*)

Page 81

The etymology of Cams Hall is quoted from *Hampshire Place-Names*,
Richard Coates (Ensign, Southampton 1989).

Page 89

The quote at the top of the page is a translation of a transmission
from a German bomber approaching Portsmouth, 17th April 1941.
The quote and subsequent information on decoy fires and an
account of the foiled raid are in:
Fields of Deception—Britain's Bombing Decoys of World War II
by Colin Dobinson (Methuen, London 2000)

Page 96

"Your Fortress Amnesia" This device was planted by Will Morris.
Objectism: subject was colonised by Olson or quasi-aesthetic,
post-Olson constructs.

Police have been given a map showing holes dug at a Portsmouth children's home at
the centre of a child abuse investigation.

The map has been drawn by a former resident at Cosham's *Children's Cottage* Home.
... he has given police a map of two locations—in a wood and near an orchard—
where he says he saw 'suspicious holes dug'.

A total of 21 men and women told detectives they suffered physical and sexual
abuse as children at the home, mostly in the 1950s.

A 78-year-old woman from Devon was arrested on suspicion of indecent assault but
when police passed the file to Crown Prosecution Service lawyers they decided there
was not enough evidence to charge her.

The Portsmouth News, 7th March 2008

Ode to Oblivion

Device located in notebook dated 1978. Device is a hypnopomp or example of nulled hypnopompic speech. A force defined by its effects, it consists of desires once suppressed by the mechanism itself. Currently inactive or stilled. *Function unknown.*

Ode to Oblivion

Oh to choose to move slowly now, to
                    fall into oblivion
anchored freely by the wind and find
               the land is slightly thin
forever shadow find your home and
          see to much you can
                         condone.

Device reveals subject to be predisposed to False Landscape Syndrome (FLS), a condition in which a person's identity and relationships are affected by beliefs pertaining to the nature of landscapes and the construction of 'places' in terms of their histories, physical structure and social, economic and political functions.

"At different scales, spatial relationships can be said to mask, naturalise or mystify contradictions either between social groups with different interests or between the forces and relations of production."
Source unknown

"Inasmuch as adolescents are unable to challenge either the dominant system's imperious architecture or its deployment of signs, it is only by way of revolt that they have any prospect of recovering the world of differences—the natural, the sensory/sensual, sexuality and pleasure."

Henri Lefebvre, *The Production of Space*
(English translation by Donald Nicholson-Smith, Blackwell, 1991), p. 50.

Lightning Source UK Ltd.
Milton Keynes UK
UKOW051408180112

185589UK00001B/11/P